OUR NAMES ARE unique

Written by: Sandra Grace Walker

Illustrated by: Sharquita White & Sandra Grace Walker

Copyright © 2023 Sandra Grace Walker

All rights reserved. No part of this book may be reproduced in any form or by any electronic or mechanical, including information storage and retrieval systems, without permission in writing from the publisher, except by reviewers, who may quote brief passages in a review.

ISBN 978-1-737-1309-7-0 (Paperback Edition)
ISBN 978-1-737-1309-6-3 (Hardcover Edition)

Library of Congress Control Number
2023904030

The viewpoints, opinions and beliefs expressed herein are solely of the author. Such views, opinions and prespectives are intended to convey a life story are based on the recollections about their lives and are not intended to malign any individual, religion, ethnic group or company.

Printed and bound in the United States of America
First printing May 2023

Published by Butterfly Language Publishing
Hampstead, MD 21074

Visit www.butterflylangaugepublishing.com

 Publishing

Dedication

This book is dedicated to all the children around the world with a unique name. Your name does not define who you are, it is a part of your identity. For that reason, own it because it is yours.

I do not want it anymore!

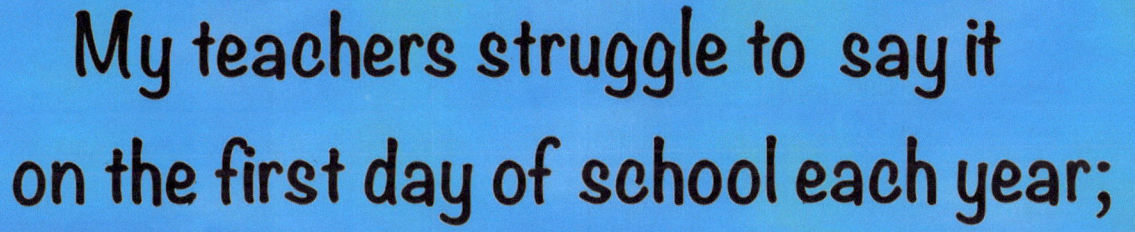

My teachers struggle to say it on the first day of school each year;

When they read our names out loud for everyone to hear.

I wish my name was different.

My wise son, do not be ashamed.

Let me tell you about your name
and the origin that it came;

It may never be personalized
unless customized on a bike plate
at a brick-and-mortar store.

It may never be written in a book by your favorite author.

But the story of your name
always makes people look,
and they get shook;

To find within your name,
that it is defined by our heritage.

Khari, Khaliq, Draya, Miyani, Draya, Symar, Syhair, Jamar, Kameia, Shanica, Sylvi, Shawntaye, Keontaye

Rafiq, Ziaire, Deoshe', Lanisha, Chaquille, Rasheeda, Zakee, Stefan, Ja'Quan, Mekhi, Diamond, Jabari, Zion, Imani, Mykera

Tyshawn, Zamairah, Samariah, Jackelys, Saleen, Khalil, Bashier, Mayasiha, Ry'anna, D'Jour, Domonique, Mathosette, Shaunna, Chakkera

Kawahn, Asinae, Chenisha, Shikeia, Dalante, Keahrie, Josenata, Nevaeh, Matiyos, Danaejah, Sheree, Jaquetta, Tychera, Keyonna, Chianti

Your name means "Like a King" and anyone can tell you what that means.

Your brother's name means creator.

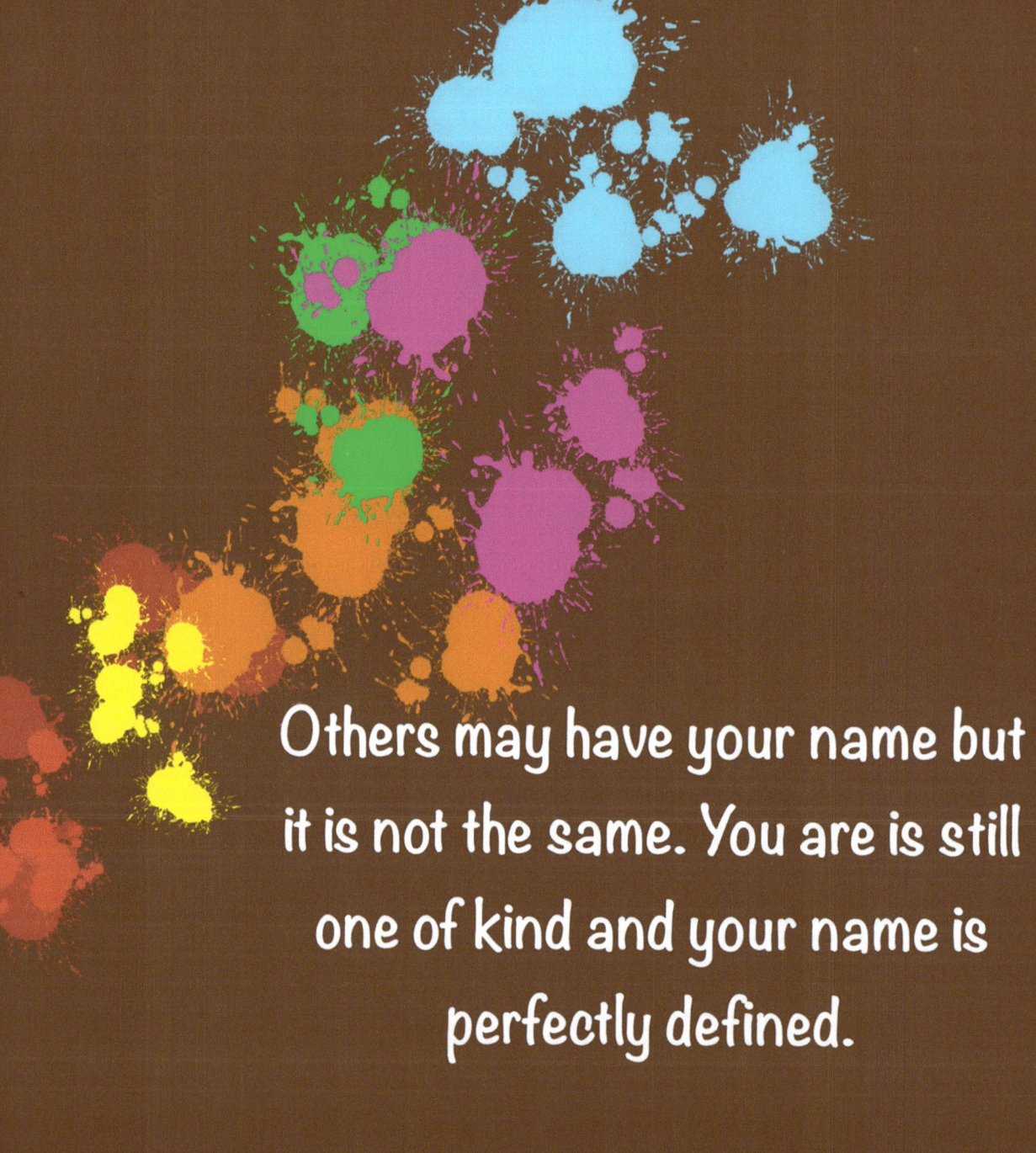

Others may have your name but it is not the same. You are is still one of kind and your name is perfectly defined.

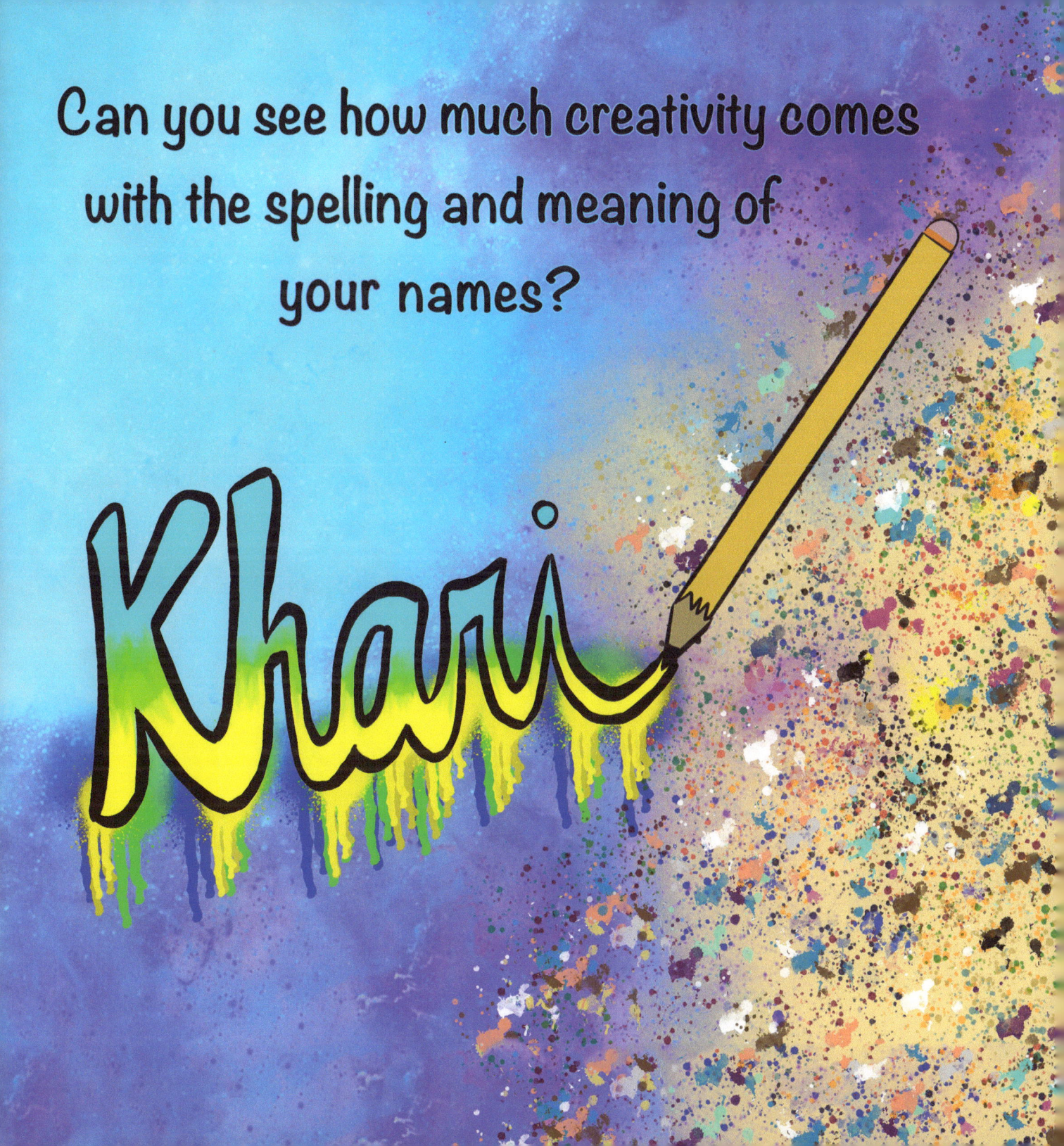

or for their religion,

Some parents combine their names to make a new name for their child.

Others may just like a name because it makes them go, wow.

Whichever way a child gets their name, trust me when I say it is thought of carefully.

So the next time your teacher struggles to speak;

Say this loud and proud with me.

My name is _____!

fill in the blank with your child name.

I am proud of my name and I will not hide it with shame.

My name is not made up...it is unique.
It is real as the words we speak.

It has a meaning, that they can't see.
So I will tell them it comes from my family tree.

But my name is special for my sake,
and I thank the creativity behind it;
the rhythm within it; the swag upon it and the soul of it.

The creation of a nation within my name is not hard to explain.

It is easy to pronounce if they just sound it out, and without a doubt, they will properly speak it out.

KHAH-REE

Call me by my name and you can see the honor bestowed upon me.

The greatest of Kings,

the excellence of thee beloved,

The majestic sounds of the heavens above it.

Can they see what my name means to me?

"But now thus saith the Lord that created thee, O Jacob, and he that formed thee, O Israel, Fear not: for I have redeemed thee, I have called thee by thy name; for thou art mine."

(Isa. 43:1 *King James Version*)

Say these affirmations aloud, so the world can feel the sound.

My name is great!
My name is unique!
My name is amazing!
My name is bold!
My name will leave an imprint on the world!
My name is a apart of my identity!
My name is me!

This children's picture book promotes self-love and hope for our brown children by letting them know that being different is beautiful.

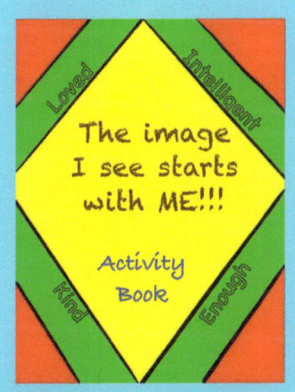

Hand drawn activity book with over 50 positive affirmations for our children to see and feel.

Black Bear Brown Cub is a rhythmic children's picture book detailing adoption process that a brown momma bear had to find a family for her young cub.

More books written by Sandra Grace Walker on sale @ Amazon.com

Stay connected with us:

butterflylanguagepublishing.com
butterflylanguagepublishing@gmail.com
https://facebook.com/sandragrace.walker
https://www.instagram.com/sandra_grace_walker

www.ingramcontent.com/pod-product-compliance
Lightning Source LLC
Chambersburg PA
CBHW041705160426
43209CB00017B/1754